BY SABRINA MESKO

HEALING MUDRAS
Yoga for Your Hands
Random House - Original edition

POWER MUDRAS
Yoga Hand Postures for Women
Random House - Original edition

MUDRA - GESTURES OF POWER
DVD - Sounds True

CHAKRA MUDRAS DVD set
HAND YOGA for Vitality, Creativity and Success
HAND YOGA for Concentration, Love and Longevity

HEALING MUDRAS
Yoga for Your Hands - New Edition

HEALING MUDRAS - New Edition in full color:
Healing Mudras I. ~ For Your Body
Healing Mudras II. ~ For Your Mind
Healing Mudras III. ~ For Your Soul

POWER MUDRAS
Yoga Hand Postures for Women - New Edition

MUDRA THERAPY
Hand Yoga for Pain Management and Conquering Illness

YOGA MIND
45 Meditations for Inner Peace, Prosperity and Protection

MUDRAS FOR ASTROLOGICAL SIGNS
Volumes I. ~ XII.
MUDRAS for ARIES, TAURUS, GEMINI, CANCER, LEO, VIRGO,
LIBRA, SCORPIO, SAGITTARIUS, CAPRICORN, AQUARIUS, PISCES
12 Book Series

LOVE MUDRAS
Hand Yoga for Two

MUDRAS AND CRYSTALS
The Alchemy of Energy Protection

THE HOLISTIC CAREGIVER
A Guidebook for at-home care in late stage of Alzheimer's and dementia

MUDRAS
for
GEMINI

By Sabrina Mesko Ph.D.H.

The material contained in this book has been written for informational purposes and is not intended as a substitute for medical advice nor is it intended to diagnose, treat, cure, or prevent disease. If you have a medical issue or illness, consult a qualified physician.

A Mudra Hands™ Book
Published by Mudra Hands Publishing

Copyright © 2013 Sabrina Mesko Ph.D.H.

Photography by Mara
Animal photography by Sabrina Mesko
Illustrations by Kiar Mesko
Cover photo by Mara

Printed in the United States of America

ISBN-13:978-0615918532
ISBN-10: 0615918530

All rights reserved. No part of this book may be reproduced or transmitted in any form or by any means, electronic or mechanical, including photocopying, recording, or by any information storage and retrieval system, without the prior written permission from the Publisher.

For all my Gemini Friends

Table of Contents

Acknowledgments	9
Introduction	12
MUDRA	16
Instructions for Practice	16
Breath Control	17
Chakras	18
Nadis	21
Your Hands and Fingers	22
Mantra	22
About Astrology	23
Your Sun Sig	24
Your Rising Sign	25
How to use this book	25
MUDRAS for TRANSCENDING CHALLENGES	27
MUDRA for Contentment	28
MUDRA for Relaxation and Joy	30
MUDRA for Protection	32
MUDRAS for Your HEALTH AND BEAUTY	35
MUDRA for Uplifting Your Heart	36
MUDRA for Diminishing Worries	38
MUDRA for Healthy Breast	40
MUDRAS for LOVE	43
MUDRA of Two Hearts	44
MUDRA for Healing Your Heart Chakra	46
MUDRA of Right Speech	48
MUDRAS for SUCCESS	51
MUDRA for Self-Confidence	52
MUDRA for Powerful Insight	54
MUDRA for Sharp Mind	56
About the Author	59

The Mudra practice is a complimentary healing technique, that offers fast and effective positive results.

Mudras work harmoniously with other traditional, alternative and complementary healing protocols.

They help restore depleted subtle energy states and optimize the practitioner's overall state of wellness.

Mudras for GEMINI

May 22 - June 21

BODY
Shoulders, lungs, arms
nervous system

PLANET
Mercury

COLORS
Yellow, orange

ELEMENT
Air

STONES and GEMS
Agate

ANIMAL
Small bird, butterfly, monkey

Introduction

Ever since I can remember, I have been fascinated by the never ending view of the stars in the sky and the presence of other mysterious planets. As a child I wondered for hours about where does the Universe end and when my Father explained the possibility that time and space exist in a very different way than we imagined, my mind went wild with possibilities. I was however quite skeptical about astrology in general until one day in my early youth, a dear friend introduced me to a true Master of Vedic Astrology. He quickly and completely diminished any of my doubts about how precise certain facts can be revealed in one's Celestial map.

It was as if an invisible veil had been removed, and I was granted a peek over to the other side. The astrologer also adamantly pointed out that nothing is written in stone and one's destiny has a lot of space to navigate thru. You can make the best of the situation if you know your given parameters. My fascination and use of astrological science continues to this day and compliments and enriches my work with other observation techniques that I use when consulting.

One is born with character aspects and potential for realization of mapped-out future events, but there is always a possibility that another road may be taken. This has to do with the choices we make. Free will is given to all of us, even though often the choices we have seem to be very limited. But still, the choices are always there, forcing us to consciously participate and eventually take responsibility for our decisions, actions, and consequences.

The science of Astrology has been around for millenniums and even though some people are still doubtful, I always remind them that there is no disputing the fact, that the Moon affects the high and low tide of our Oceans - hence our bodies consisting mostly of water are affected by planetary movements in many fascinating and profound ways. Even the biggest skeptic agrees with that fact.

The Love of the Universal Power for each one of us is unconditional, everlasting and omnipresent. No matter what kind of life-journey you have, it is the very best one designed especially for you, rest assured. And when you are experiencing life's various challenges and wishing for a smooth ride instead, keep in mind that a life filled with lessons is a life fulfilling its purpose. The tests you encounter in your daily life are your opportunities. The wisdom learned is your asset, and the experiences gained are your wealth. Your Spirit's abundance is measured by the battles you fought and how you fought them. Did you help others and leave this world a better place in any way? Your true intention matters more than you know.

Each one of us has a very unique-one of a kind celestial map placed gently, but firmly and irrevocably into effect at the precise time of our birth. There are certain aspects of one's chart that reveal possible character tendencies and predisposed behavior in regards to love, partnerships, maintaining one's health, pursuit of success and a way of communicating. The benefits of knowing and understanding the effects of your chart on various aspects of your life can be profound. It can help you understand and prepare ahead of time for certain circumstances that are coming your way, which increases the possibility of a better quality of life in general.

If you knew that a specific time period could be beneficial for your career wouldn't it be good to know that ahead of your plans? If you are aware that certain aspects of your physical constitution are predisposed to a weakness or sensitivity, wouldn't it be beneficial to pay attention and prevent a possible future health ailment?

If you can foresee that a certain time will be slower for you in achieving positive results, wouldn't it be wise to use that time for preparation for a more fortuitous timing? How many times have you attempted to pursue a dream of yours that just didn't seem to want to happen? And when you were completely exhausted and disillusioned, the fortunate opportunity presented itself, except now you were tired, overwhelmed and had no energy or enthusiasm left. Having such information ahead of time would offer you the chance to save your energy during quiet, less active time, so that when your luck is more likely, you can seize the opportunity and make the most of it. Since writing my first books on Mudras a while ago, my work has expanded into many different areas, however I always included Mudras into my new ventures. When I designed International Wellness and Spa centers, I included Mudra programs to share these beneficial techniques with a wide audience. I included Mudras into my weekly TV show and guided large audiences thru practice on live shows.

Mudras will forever fascinate me and I have been humbled and excited how many practitioners from around the world have written me, grateful to have these techniques and most importantly really experiencing positive effects in time of need. Therefore it has been a natural idea for me to combine these two of my favorite topics and create a series of Mudra sets for all twelve Astrological signs.

The Mudras depicted in this book are specifically selected for the astrological sign of Aries with intention to help you maximize your gifts and soften the challenges that your celestial map contains.

It is important to know that each astrological chart - celestial map-contains information that can be used beneficially and there are no "bad signs" or "better sings". Your chart is unique as are you. By gaining information, knowledge and understanding what the placements of the planets offer you, your path to self knowledge is strengthened.

I hope this book will attract astrology readers as well as meditation and yoga practitioners and help you utilize the beneficial combination of both these fascinating techniques. Knowledge will help you experience the very best possible version of your life. The biggest mystery in your life is You. Discover who you are and enjoy the journey.

And remember, no matter what life presents you with, don't forget to smile and keep a happy heart. With each experience gained you are spiritually wealthier for it. And that my friend, stays with you forever.

The wisdom gained is eternally imprinted in your soul.

Blessings,

Sabrina

MUDRAS

Mudras are movements involving only fingers, hands and arms. Mudras originated in ancient Egypt where they were practiced by high priests and priestesses in sacred rituals. Mudras can be found in every culture of the world. We all use Mudras in our everyday life when gesturing while communicating and when holding our hands in various intuitive positions. Mudras used in yoga practice offer great benefits and have a tremendously positive overall effect on our overall state of well-being. By connecting specific fingertips and your palms in various Mudra positions, you are directly affecting complex energy currents of your subtle energy body. As numerous energy currents run thru your brain centers, Mudras help stimulate specific areas for an overall state of emotional, physical and mental well being.

Instructions for Mudra Practice

YOUR BODY POSTURE
During the Mudra practice sit in an upright position with a straight spine, with both your feet on the ground or in a cross legged position. Comfort is essential so that you may practice undisturbed and focus on proper practice positions.

YOUR EYES
Keep your eyes closed and gently lightly lift the gaze above the horizon.

WHERE
For achieving best results of ideal Mudra practice it is essential that you find a peaceful place, without distractions. Once your Mudra practice is established, you can practice Mudras anywhere.

WHEN
You may practice Mudras at any time. Best times for practice are first thing in the morning and at bedtime. Avoid practicing Mudras on a full stomach, and after a big meal wait for an hour before practice.

HOW LONG
Each Mudra should be practiced for at least 3 minutes at a time. Ideal practice is 3 Mudras for 3 minutes each with a follow up short 3 minutes of complete stillness, peace and meditation or reflection.

HOW OFTEN
You may practice Mudras every day. Explore various Mudras by selecting a Mudra that fits your specific needs for any given day.

BREATH CONTROL
Proper breathing is essential for optimal Mudra practice. There are two main breathing techniques that can be used with your practice.

LONG DEEP SLOW BREATH
Slowly and deeply inhale thru your nose while relaxing and expanding the area or your solar plexus and lower stomach. Exhale thru the nose slowly while gently contracting the stomach area and pulling your stomach in. Pace your breathing slowly and notice the immediate calming effects. This breathing technique is appropriate for relaxation, inducing calmness and peace.

BREATH OF FIRE
Inhale and exhale thru the nose at a much faster pace while practicing the same concept of expanding navel area and contracting with each exhalation. Unless otherwise noted Mudras are generally practiced with the long slow breath. The breath of fire has an energizing, recharging effect on body and is to be used only when so noted.

Chakras

Along our spine, starting at the base and continuing up towards the top of your head, lie subtle energy centers-vortexes-called charkas, that have a powerful effect on the overall state of your health and well being.
The practice of Mudras profoundly affects the proper function of these energy centers and magnifies their power.

Our subtle energy body is highly sensitive to outside sensory stimuli of sound, aromas, visuals and outside electric currents that constantly surround us. Frequencies that permeate specific locations may attract or bother you. Perhaps you may feel eager to stay somewhere where the energy suits you and yet feel suffocated when the environment does not agree with you. We are all sensitive to energies, but some of us feel them more than others.

A positive blend of energies with another person can create a magnet-like effect, whereas another person's negative unharmonious subtle energy field subconsciously pushes you away.

By leading healthy lives and optimizing the proper function of charkas, you empower your subtle energy bodies adding strength to your physical body, mind and spirit. Destructive behavior like addictions and abuse weakens your Auric field and "leaks" your vital energy. By maintaining a healthy Aura-energy field, you can fine-tune your natural capacity for "sensing" places, situations and people that compliment your energy frequency.
In a state of "clean energy" you achieve capacity for high awareness and become your own best guide.

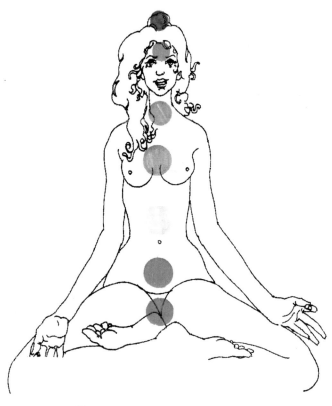

CHAKRAS IN THE BODY

Base Chakra: Foundation
Second Chakra: Sexuality
Third Chakra: Ego
Fourth Chakra: Love
Fifth Chakra: Truth
Sixth Chakra: Intuition
Seventh Chakra: Divine Wisdom

FIRST CHAKRA
LOCATION: Base of the spine
GLAND: Gonad
COLOR: Red
REPRESENTS:
Foundation, shelter, survival,
courage, inner security, vitality

SECOND CHAKRA
LOCATION: Sex organs
GLAND: Adrenal
COLOR: Orange
REPRESENTS:
Creative expression, sexuality,
procreation, family

THIRD CHAKRA
LOCATION: Solar plexus
GLAND: Pancreas
COLOR: Yellow
REPRESENTS:
Ego, intellect, emotions of fear and anger

FOURTH CHAKRA
LOCATION: Heart
GLAND: Thymus
COLOR: Green
REPRESENTS:
All matters of the heart, love,
self–love, compassion and faith

FIFTH CHAKRA
LOCATION: Throat
GLAND: Thyroid
COLOR: Blue
REPRESENTS:
Communication, truth,
higher knowledge, your voice

SIXTH CHAKRA
LOCATION: Third Eye
GLAND: Pineal
COLOR: Indigo
REPRESENTS:
Intuition, inner vision, the Third eye

SEVENTH CHAKRA
LOCATION: Top of the head - Crown
GLAND: Pituitary
COLOR: White and Violet
REPRESENTS:
The universal God consciousness,
the heavens, unity

NADIS

Your subtle energy body contains an amazing network of electric currents called Nadis. There are 72.000 energy currents that run throughout your body from toes to the top of your head as well as your fingertips. These channels of light must be clear and vibrant with life force for your optimal health and empowerment. With regular Mudra practice you can open, clear, reactivate and re-energize your energy currents.

Your Hands and Fingers

While practicing Mudras you are magnifying the effects of the Solar system on your physical, mental and spiritual body. Each finger is influenced by the following planets:

THE THUMB - MARS

THE INDEX FINGER - JUPITER

THE MIDDLE FINGER - SATURN

THE RING FINGER – THE SUN

THE LITTLE FINGER - MERCURY

MANTRA

Combining the Mudra practice with appropriate Mantras magnifies the beneficial effects of these ancient self-healing techniques.

The hard palate in your mouth has 58 energy meridian points that connect to and affect your entire body.

By singing, speaking or whispering Mantras, you touch these energy points in a specific order that is beneficial and has a harmonious and healing effect on your physical, mental and spiritual state.

The ancient science of Mantras helps you reactivate nadis, magnifies and empowers your energy field, improves your concentration and stills your mind.

About Astrology

The word Horoscope originates from a Latin word ORA–hour and SCOPOS–view. One could presume that Horoscope means "a look into your hour of birth". The precise moment of your birth determines your celestial set-up.

An accurate astrological chart can reveal most detailed aspects of your life, your character, your gifts, your future possible events, challenges that await you, lucky events that are bestowed upon you, and your outlook for happy relationships, successful careers, accomplishments, health and many possible variations of life events. I say possible, because your decisions will determine the outcome.

There are 12 signs in the Zodiac and your birth-day reflects the position of your Sun sign. The specific positions of other planets in your chart are calculated considering the precise moment-hour and minute and of course location of your birth. The birth time will reveal your Rising or Ascending sign, which will further determine other essential facts of your chart.

The constant transitional movements of the Planets affect each one of us differently, a time that may be difficult for some may prove supremely lucky for another and yet we are interconnected by mutual effects of continuous planetary movements. Nothing is standing still, the changes are ongoing. On a different note, a few slow moving planets connect us in other ways, as they keep certain generations under specific aspects and influences. We are all inseparable and in continuous motion.

There are numerous fascinating ways to use astrology and there is no doubt that the constant motion of all these powerful and majestic Planets in our Solar system affect each and every one of us differently. Astrology can be used as an additional tool to help you continue progressing on the mysterious life journey of self discovery and self-realization.

Remember, the power of decision is yours as is the responsibility for consequences. Make peace with your doubts, pursue your dreams and relish in results.

When the outcome is less than what you expected, learn to pick yourself up and continue on, wiser with knowledge you gained, that alone being a good reason for remaining optimistic. When the outcome surpasses your expectations, well, then you will know what to do… mostly take a breath, smile, and enjoy the moment.

Your Sun Sign

There are 12 signs in the Zodiac. The day of your birth determines your Sun-sign. Most often this is the extent of average person's knowledge and interest in astrology. However, the other aspects in the astrological chart are equally as important and need to be taken into consideration. In this book your main guide is your Sun sign's dispositions, tendencies, weaknesses and gifts. Certainly there are endless combinations of charts and your Sun sign alone will not reveal the complete picture of your celestial map.

For more detailed information and reflection about your chart, you need to know your ascending-rising sign.

Your Ascending-Rising Sign

Your rising sign, also known as the ascendant, reflects the degree of ecliptic rising over the eastern horizon at the precise moment of your birth. It reveals the foundation of your personality. That means that even if you have the same birthday with someone else, your time of birth would create completely different aspects and influences in your chart. No two people are alike. You are one of a kind and so is everyone else. However, you may have some strong similarities and timing aspects that will be often alike. Your rising sign also reveals the basis of your chart and House placements. Your rising sign determines and is in your first house. There are 12 Houses and each depicts precise in-depth information about all aspects of your physical life, emotional make and character tendencies. It is incredibly complex and fascinating. Regarding your Mudra practice in combination with your Astrological Sign, it would be beneficial to know also your Rising sign and apply Mudras that empower your Rising sign as well. For example; if your Sun sign is Aries, but your rising sign is Libra-it would be most beneficial to practice Mudra sets for both signs.

How to use this book

In each book of the *Mudras for the Astrological Signs* series, you will find Mudras for different astrological signs that will help you in most important areas of your life: Health, Love, Success, and Overcoming your challenging qualities. We all have them, as we also all have gifts. This book is specific for the sign of Aries. You may change your Mudra practice daily as needed, and keep in mind, that certain habits or tendencies need a longer time to adjust, change, and improve. Be patient, kind, and loving towards yourself.

Mudras for Transcending Challenges

Each one of us has a few character tendencies or weaknesses that are connected to our astrological chart. To help you transcend, overcome and redirect these challenges into your beneficial assets, you can use the Mudras in this chapter.

Mudras for Health and Beauty

Each astrological sign rules certain areas of your body. The Mudras in this chapter will help you strengthen your physical weaknesses while maintaining a healthy body, and a beautiful, vibrant appearance.

Mudras for Love

The Mudras in this chapter will help you understand your love temperament, your expectations, your longings and how to attract the optimal love partner into your life. It is most beneficial to know how others perceive you in the matters of the heart. It will also help you understand your partner and their astrologically influenced love map.

Mudras for Success

The Mudras in this chapter will offer you tools to present yourself to the world in your optimal light. Often one is confused in which direction to turn or where their strength lies. Mudras will help you focus and remember your essential creative desires, help you gain self-confidence and inner security to recognize your desired and destined path. If you know what you want, and your purpose is harmonious for the better good of all, your success is within reach.

MUDRAS for TRANSCENDING CHALLENGES

MUDRA FOR CONTENTMENT

There are two people inside of you and that offers more gifts and benefits, but also creates some inner friction. You are "talented for two" and therefore the inner dialogue needs more attention and discipline. If you ignore this aspects, you will experience some kind of inexplicable discontent when everything is wonderful, and often a wavering of moods for no reason. Understanding yourself and this aspect is most important, and yet, balancing your powerful inner energies requires more work and time. This Mudra is very beneficial for taming these aspects and should be practiced daily. Then, your two "Inner artists" will live in peace and everlasting harmony.

CHAKRA: 3
COLOR: Yellow
MANTRA:
**SARE SA SA SARE
SA SA SARE HARE HAR**
(God Is Infinite in His Creativity)

Sit with a straight back and lift your hands in front of your stomach area. Connect your thumb and the middle finger of the right hand and the thumb and the little finger of the left hand. Relax the rest of the fingers and hold your hands a few inches apart, palms up. Hold for three minutes, the make fists with both hands and relax.

BREATH: Long, deep and slow.

MUDRA FOR RELAXATION AND JOY

Your restless spirit and creative ideas are alive and active in every moment of your day. Taking a real relaxing vacation with no other purposeful activity does not appeal to you. Being the social butterfly that you are, you often miss the perfect opportunity to relax and just be-a very necessary and vital part of creative process. Once you allow yourself to take a breather and look at the ocean or the sunset, your mood is instantly uplifted, your ideas soar and you are renewed and truly happy. This Mudra will help you accomplish that, even when you do not have the luxury of an amazing environment. Just close your eyes and transport yourself wherever your heart desires, but be still, breathe and experience the true meaning of relaxation.

CHAKRA : 3, 4

COLOR: Yellow, green

MANTRA:

HAREE HAR HAREE HAR
(God in His Creative Aspect)

Sit with a straight back, lift up your hands up in front of your chest. Make a fist with your left hand, tucking the thumb inside. Wrap the right hand around the left and place your right thumb over the base of the left thumb. Concentrate on your third Eye area and hold for three minutes. Later, extend your practice to eleven minutes.

BREATH: Long, deep and slow.

MUDRA
FOR PROTECTION

With your generous and happy heart you may often forget to practice any caution. You may just trust that this world is perfect, pure, and everyone is harmless. Become more aware of other people's mindset, motivations and tendencies to take advantage of anyone who allows it. It does not mean looking at everyone and everything with suspicion, it only means to be aware, and do not give away the last thing you have just because someone asks you too. Learn to look out for yourself with discipline and caution. To protect yourself from any negative people, situations or circumstances, practice this Mudra, stay calm and focused. This world is an adventure, but it is also a jungle that needs to be walked thru with caution.

CHAKRA: All chakras

COLOR: All colors

MANTRA:

OM

(God Is His Absolute State)

Sit with a straight spine. Cross your left hand over your right one and place them on your upper chest. Palms are facing you and all fingers are together. Hold for three minutes and feel the immediate energy shift.

BREATH: Long, deep and slow.

MUDRAS for HEALTH and BEAUTY

MUDRA FOR UPLIFTING YOUR HEART

Sensitive that you are, you need to take care of your heart, so that your feelings and emotions do not take you into dark waters of gloom. Then it seems like your other twin sowed up-and we don't really want him/her do we? By being aware that you are extra sensory gifted and at the same time delicate, you need to take good care of your body-instrument and protect your gifts. Pleasant, calm environment and people are a must and no emotional stress should be allowed for too long. Often life takes us into directions we never expected, and tests us precisely in areas of our weakness, thus your prompt awareness is of great importance. Guard your inner peace and heart each and every day.

CHAKRA : 4

COLOR: Green

Sit with a straight back, and lift up your arms shoulder level, elbows bent and parallel to the ground. Tuck your thumbs under your armpits and keep the rest of your fingers straight and together. Your hands should be above your breasts, palms facing down. As you inhale, the distance between the middle fingertips gets bigger; as you exhale, the middle fingertips should touch or cross each other. With each inhalation feel the healing energy expand your heart and chest area. Continue for three minutes and relax.

BREATH: Long, deep and slow.

MUDRA FOR DIMINISHING WORRIES

You are very youthful and adaptable and may give an appearance of lightheartedness and a carefree disposition, but deep inside, you tend to worry and are quite restless. This of course is not constructive, productive or healthy. Learn to do your best and then truly let go and let Universe work to your benefit. This Mudra will help you release the worry habit and establish a state of calm inner peace, so that you can visualize and attract positive outcomes, developments and people into your life.

CHAKRA: 4, 5, 6

COLOR: Green, blue, indigo

Sit with a straight back. Bring your hands in front of your chest with the palms facing up. The sides of the little fingers and inner sides of the palms are touching. Now bring the middle fingertips together, perpendicular to the palms. Extend the thumbs away from the palm. Hold and keep the fingers stretched as little antennas for energy.

BREATH: Long, deep and slow.

MUDRA FOR HEALTHY BREAST AND HEART

Your vulnerable areas of heart, lungs, respiration and chest area require your care and attention. That encompasses all levels of special care: physical, mental and emotional. Releasing challenging emotions associated with matters of heart and positive mental dispositions in relation to these aspects as well. Extra physical care is required to assure long lasting health of this region, breathing exercise in the open are ideal. Regular practice of this Mudra will help you keep your chest area clear of dense negative energy, and continuously recharged with new vital life force.

CHAKRA: 4

COLOR: Green

Sit with a straight back. Relax your arms at your sides with the palms facing forward. Then alternatively bend each elbow so that the forearms come toward the heart center as rapidly as possible. When your right hand is at your chest, the left hand is away from the body and when the left hand is at your chest, the right hand is away from the body. Do not bend the wrists or hands and do not touch the chest. Continue at a rapid pace four times while you inhale, four times while you exhale, until you feel hot, then relax for a few minutes.

BREATH: Long, deep and slow.

MUDRAS for LOVE

MUDRA OF TWO HEARTS

You are quite the lively, witty romantic, and it may be very clear in your mind and heart who the love of your life is, but your other "invisible twin" may give out different signals all together. Appearing non-committal in matters of the heart will create some understandable frustration and heartache for your partner. That is why it is ever important for you to expand your thinking, communication habits, perception, and awaken your awareness of your partner and the consequences of your perhaps tackless actions. Your lover needs assurance that your temporary doubts have nothing to do with them, but your inner restlessness. To help you achieve and maintain harmony in love, practice this Mudra and focus on aligning your energy and needs with that of your lover. The temporary "hick-up" will pass and all will be well again in your land of love.

CHAKRA : 4

COLOR: Green

MANTRA:
SAT NAM

(Truth Is God's Name, One in Spirit)

Sit with a straight spine. Connect the thumbs and index fingers on each hand and spread out and extend all other fingers. Lift your arms in front of your heart, cross arms in front of you - left in front of right, palms facing out. Little fingers are hooked onto each other. Keep fingers nice and extended thru the practice.

BREATH: Long, deep and slow.

MUDRA FOR HEALING YOUR HEART CHAKRA

You are very charming and desirable, but there will be times when like the rest of us, you will need to learn a few love lessons. For example; how forgetting your lovers birthday is a bad idea, or how shyness doesn't always pay off, and how sometimes taking responsibility for your actions or words is the best way to resolve an unnecessary conflict. On the other hand, you may need to heal your heart when hurt by someone who simply does not understand your sensitive nature. It is most important that you learn how to strengthen and protect your heart and navigate thru the love and romance process with some confidence and lightness. Your perfect mate will appear when the time is perfect. And that is not up to you, so just breathe, relax, and keep your heart harmonious and loving, always open to new adventures.

CHAKRA : 4

COLOR: Green

Sit with a straight spine. Lift your right hand up, elbow bent, your hand at the level of your face. Make a fist and leave only the index finger extended, pointing up. Place your left hand on your chest above your breast, elbow parallel to the ground. Hold and feel the energy shifting in your body. Keep the elbows nice and high.

BREATH: Long, deep and slow.

MUDRA FOR RIGHT SPEECH

Some people prefer very demonstrative and open verbal communication of love and affection. This is where you may run into some challenges-a light, harmless joke may be misunderstood, a simple expression of fear of commitment may send your lover into a state of distress. Some of us are more sensitive than others, and while you are sensitive yourself, you are less cautious with what you express. Not to worry, just pay a tiny bit more attention when talking about the matters of the heart-your lover hangs on every word and it will really brighten their day, if you gift them with a romantic expression and gesture, tell a few sweet words, and make them feel they are in heaven - after all, you are a very romantic partner who needs and loves being a team. Tell them so.

CHAKRA : 3, 5

COLOR: Yellow, blue

MANTRA:
HAR DHAM HAR HAR
(God is the Creator)

Sit with a straight spine. Relax your arms, keep your elbows at your sides, and bring your hands up in front of your stomach, palms open and flat, facing up. Spread your fingers gently and touch the tips of the ring fingers together, the right little finger is under the left little finger. Now concentrate and tense the thumb and the index fingers without moving the fingers. Hold for a few seconds and release. Now tense the thumb and the middle fingers, again without moving. Hold for a few seconds and release. Next tense the thumb and the ring fingers. Hold and release. Lastly, tense the thumb and little fingers, hold for a few seconds and relax. Repeat the cycle reversing the little fingers.

BREATH: Long, deep and slow.

MUDRAS for SUCCESS

MUDRA FOR SELF-CONFIDENCE

There is a real genius inside of you and many are aware if it, but this world still requires for you to come out of your creative space and confidently express who you are. Your inner wavering and indecisive nature may present an obstacle when you are on your way to the top. This demands some inner work on your part. Establishing a strong sense of confidence before exposing yourself to the world, where there will be praise but also naturally criticism-this requires a strong confident persona. You can have all that and more, but work at it. Do not dismiss this detail, for it is the total of all elements that creates success, genius alone won't do. After all, this is planet Earth and you can't be in the clouds all the time. Stand strong and confident on the ground and your will be rewarded.

CHAKRA : 3, 6

COLOR: Yellow, indigo

MANTRA:
**EK ONG KAR SAT GURU PRASAD
SAT GURU PRASAD EK ONG KAR**

(The Creator Is the One That Dispels Darkness and Illuminates Us by His Grace)

Sit with a straight back. Lift your hands up to the level of your solar plexus with elbows bent to the sides. Bend the middle, ring, and little fingers and touch them back to back. Extend the index fingers and thumbs and press them together. The thumbs are pointed toward you and the index fingers away from you.

BREATH: Long, deep and slow.

MUDRA FOR POWERFUL INSIGHT

As a versatile intellectual and eloquent individual it is understandably challenging when outside demands start interfering with your pure creative spirit. But the mastery of success requires your capacity to be adaptable and manage to find that fine-tuned balance between what brings you joy and what also works for your to finally enjoy the fruits of your labor. Everyone has to adapt a bit, to better convey their message. Do not take this personally, take it as a necessary element of the process. This Mudra will help you find that perfect combination and blend the magical elements that can be fine-tuned and finally presented in such a fashion that it will absolutely work. Take your time and reflect, it is as important as all other steps on this journey.

CHAKRA : 6

COLOR: Indigo

MANTRA:
SAT NAM
(Truth is God's Name, One in Spirit)

Sit with a straight back, elbows out to either side. Raise your hands until they meet above the navel point. The back of the left hand rests in the right palm and the thumbs are crossed, left over right.

BREATH: Long, deep and slow.

MUDRA FOR A SHARP MIND

When time for action is here, you need to be equipped to act quickly, decisively and confidently. That is not always the easiest challenge. Any kind of wavering can cost you a golden opportunity. In moments like this, take your time and practice this Mudra to achieve a state of a sharp mind where the ideas are clear as a whistle and the final picture is set in your mind. Once you have achieved that state, there will be no stopping you and you will be heard, seen and paid attention too. Much earned success will arrive!

CHAKRA : 3, 6

COLOR: Yellow, Indigo

MANTRA:
HARA HARE HARI
(The Creator in Action)

Sit with a straight spine. Hold the left hand up in front of you chest as if ready to clap, then with an extended index and middle finger of your right hand firmly walk up the center of the left palm, starting at the bottom of the palm and continuing to the very tips of middle and ring fingers of the left hand. Walk up and down your palm while maintaining pressure.

BREATH: Long, deep and slow.

ABOUT THE AUTHOR

SABRINA MESKO PH.D.H. is an International and Los Angeles Times bestselling author of the timeless classic *Healing Mudras - Yoga for your Hands* translated into fourteen languages. She authored over twenty books on Mudras, Mudra Therapy, Mudras and Astrology, Holistic Caregiving, Spirituality and Meditation techniques.

Sabrina holds a Bachelors Degree in Sensory Approaches to Healing, a Masters in Holistic Science, a Doctorate in Ancient and Modern Approaches to Healing, and a Ph.D.H in Healtheoloyy from the American Institute of Holistic Theology. She is board certified from the American Alternative medical Association and American Holistic Health Association. She has been featured in media outlets such as The Los Angeles Times, CNBC News, Cosmopolitan, the cover of London Times Lifestyle, The Discovery Channel documentary on Hands, W magazine, First for Women, Health, Web-MD, Daily News, Focus, Yoga Journal, Australian Women's weekly, Blend, Daily Breeze, New Age, the Roseanne Show and various international live television programs. Her articles have been published in world-wide publications. She hosted her own weekly TV show educating about health, well-being and complementary medicine. She is an executive member of the World Yoga Council and has led numerous international Yoga Therapy educational programs. She directed and produced her interactive double DVD titled *Chakra Mudras* - a Visionary awards finalist.

Sabrina also created award winning international Spa and Wellness Centers and is a motivational keynote conference speaker addressing large audiences all over the world. She is the founder of Arnica Press, a boutique Book Publishing House. Her mission is to discover, mentor, nurture and publish unique authors with a meaningful message, that may otherwise not have an opportunity to be heard. She is the founder of world's only online Mudra Teacher and Mudra Therapy Education, Certification and Mentorship program, with her certified therapists spreading these ancient teachings in over 27 countries around the world.

www.SabrinaMesko.com

Made in United States
North Haven, CT
03 December 2022

27662007R00035